TRANSFORM YOUR ENTERPRISE WITH GENERATIVE AI

Harnessing Generative AI
For Transformative Business Growth

RAJIV TULSYAN

Made with ❤ on the Notion Press Platform
www.notionpress.com

Dedication

To my parents, Shri Ram Niranjan Tulsayan and Smt. Maya Devi, whose unwavering support and guidance have been the foundation of my journey.

To my loving wife, Mrs. Priyanka Tulsyan, whose encouragement and understanding have been my pillars of strength.

And to my precious children, Ansh & Aarush, who inspire me every day with their joy and innocence.

This book is dedicated to you, my cherished family, for being the heartbeat of my life and the driving force behind my endeavors. Your love fuels my passion, and your presence is the greatest gift. Thank you for being my constant source of inspiration and for sharing this incredible journey with me.

About the Author

Rajiv Tulsyan is an accomplished Solutions Architect with a distinguished career spanning over two decades, marked by a proven track record in architecting distributed systems and driving enterprise-level technology roadmaps on a global scale.

His expertise encompasses a spectrum of skills, from designing and building accelerators, to a deep understanding of SOA, Event Driven, and Microservices event-based architecture. Rajiv's mastery extends to cloud technologies, including Hybrid Cloud Architecture and managed services, coupled with proficiency in Java, Kubernetes, Docker, and API gateway technologies.

As the Solutions Architect, he is currently steering the design of architecture strategies for large-scale application deployments, showcasing his commitment to scalable, resilient, and innovative solutions.

With an academic background featuring an MS in Consulting Management and an MCA in Computer Application, Rajiv Tulsyan has seamlessly blended theoretical knowledge with practical application throughout his career. His commitment to excellence is underscored by certifications such as TOGAF 9.2 Enterprise Architecture, positioning him as a thought leader in the field.

Contact this self-driven, competent, and amazing team player at mailto:info@rajivtulsyan.com. You can also get in touch with him at https://www.linkedin.com/in/rajiv-tulsyan-1511a123/

Contents

DEDICATION 3

ABOUT THE AUTHOR 4

LIST OF FIGURES 10

LIST OF TABLES 11

CHAPTER 1: UNDERSTANDING GENERATIVE AI 12

    KEY CONCEPTS AND TERMINOLOGY 12

    HISTORICAL PERSPECTIVE AND EVOLUTION 14

    THE IMPACT OF GENERATIVE AI ON BUSINESS 15

    CASE STUDIES AND REAL-WORLD EXAMPLES 18

    FUTURE TRENDS AND CHALLENGES 28

CHAPTER 2: TYPES OF GENERATIVE AI MODELS 30

    GENERATIVE ADVERSARIAL NETWORKS (GANs) 30

    GAN ARCHITECTURE 30

    TRAINING PROCESS 31

    REAL-WORLD APPLICATIONS 32

    TRANSFORMERS 32

    TRANSFORMER ARCHITECTURE 33

    APPLICATIONS IN BUSINESS 34

    VARIATIONAL AUTOENCODERS (VAEs) 35

    HOW VAEs WORK 35

    APPLICATIONS IN BUSINESS 35

    OTHER GENERATIVE MODELS 37

    CHOOSING THE RIGHT MODEL FOR YOUR BUSINESS NEEDS 37

CHAPTER 3: BUSINESS APPLICATIONS OF GENERATIVE AI 39

CONTENT CREATION AND AUTOMATION...39

AUTOMATED CONTENT GENERATION...39

REPORT GENERATION 40

TEXT GENERATION 40

CHATBOTS AND VIRTUAL ASSISTANTS..40

CONTENT GENERATION 40

IMAGE AND VIDEO SYNTHESIS...41

IMAGE ENHANCEMENT...41

VIDEO CONTENT CREATION...41

AUDIO AND MUSIC GENERATION 41

MUSIC COMPOSITION 42

VOICEOVERS 42

ENHANCING USER EXPERIENCES...42

PERSONALIZATION AND RECOMMENDATION SYSTEMS.........................42

USER INTERFACE DESIGN 43

DATA AUGMENTATION AND ANALYSIS...43

DATA AUGMENTATION...43

ANOMALY DETECTION...43

PREDICTIVE ANALYTICS..44

CASE STUDIES AND REAL-WORLD EXAMPLES......................................45

CHAPTER 4: ENHANCING INNOVATION WITH GENERATIVE AI.............. 54

HOW GENERATIVE AI SPURS INNOVATION 54

THE ROLE OF AI IN THE CREATIVE PROCESS 56

HUMAN-AI COLLABORATION..56

CASE STUDIES AND REAL-WORLD EXAMPLES......................................57

Promoting a Culture of Innovation 62

Overcoming Creative Challenges with AI 63

Case Studies and Real-World Examples....................64

CHAPTER 5: IMPROVING MARKETING ENGAGEMENT 69

AI-Powered Marketing Campaigns...........................69

Personalization and Targeting 72

Tailored Content and Offers 72

Chatbots and Virtual Assistants...........................74

Social Media and Content Optimization...................75

Measuring ROI and Effectiveness..........................76

Appendix: Data and Statistics..............................77

CHAPTER 6: STREAMLINING OPERATIONS AND EFFICIENCY 81

Automating Routine Tasks...................................81

Supply Chain Optimization 82

Complex Supply Chains......................................82

Applications and Benefits 82

Predictive Maintenance 85

Inventory and Demand Forecasting 87

Cost Reduction and Resource Allocation 87

CHAPTER 7: DATA-DRIVEN DECISION MAKING 89

Leveraging AI for Data Analysis...........................89

Predictive Analytics and Business Intelligence 91

Business Intelligence/Data Visualization 92

Risk Management and Fraud Detection.......................92

How AI Contributed to the Reduction in Fraud.............97

CHAPTER 8: ETHICAL CONSIDERATIONS IN AI **103**

BIAS AND FAIRNESS IN AI 103

STRATEGIES TO ENSURE FAIRNESS 105

DATA PRIVACY AND SECURITY 105

ETHICAL AI USE IN BUSINESS 107

LEGAL AND REGULATORY FRAMEWORKS 108

REGULATORY REQUIREMENTS 108

BUILDING TRUST WITH STAKEHOLDERS 110

CASE STUDIES AND REAL-WORLD EXAMPLES 111

PARTNER TRUST 115

CHAPTER 9: IMPLEMENTING GENERATIVE AI **116**

DEVELOPING AN AI STRATEGY 116

ALIGNING AI WITH BUSINESS GOALS 118

BUILDING A CONCEPTUAL MODEL FOR AI STRATEGY 119

IDENTIFYING THE RIGHT USE CASES 120

DATA COLLECTION AND PREPARATION 121

SCALING AI ADOPTION 125

MEASURING IMPACT 126

CHAPTER 10: PREPARING FOR FUTURE OF GENERATIVE AI **127**

EMERGING TRENDS IN AI 127

FUTURE BUSINESS OPPORTUNITIES 128

AI-FIRST COMPANIES 130

THE ONGOING EVOLUTION OF AI IN BUSINESS 131

STAYING COMPETITIVE AND INNOVATIVE 132

STAYING COMPETITIVE AND INNOVATIVE 133

CONTINUOUS LEARNING 133

Embracing Lifelong Learning in the Age of AI 133

Benefits of B2B collaboration include: 136

APPENDICES **140**

Additional Resources 140

Glossary of AI Terms 140

INDEX **142**

List of Figures

Figure 1: The Impact of AI on Marketing Effectiveness........ 71

Figure 2: Conceptual Model 1 - AI-Powered Personalization

.... 73

Figure 3: Benefits of Supply Chain Optimization with AI 84

Figure 4: Conceptual Model 2 - Predictive Maintenance Process

.... 86

Figure 5: Conceptual Model 3 - Understanding Bias in AI .. 104

Figure 6: Information Sources for Regulatory Intelligence .. 109

Figure 7: Conceptual Model for Building AI Framework 119

List of Tables

Table 1: Steps to Foster a Culture of Innovation 62

Table 2: Benefits of AI-Powered Chatbots and Virtual Assistants 75

Table 3: Examples of Routine Tasks for Automation 82

Table 4: Examples of Cost Reduction Opportunities with AI 88

Table 5: Reduction in Fraudulent Transactions at JPMorgan Chase 95

Table 6: Improvement in Patient Outcomes at Mercy Health 101

Table 7: Principles of Responsible AI 107

Table 8: Use Case Selection Matrix 121

Table 9: Data Preparation Checklist 123

Table 10: Key Performance Indicators (KPIs) for AI Scaling 126

Chapter 1:

Understanding Generative AI

Generative Artificial Intelligence (AI) has emerged as a transformative force in the business world. It holds the potential to revolutionize the way organizations operate, innovate, and engage with customers.

Key Concepts and Terminology

Before delving into the specifics of Generative AI, it's essential to grasp some fundamental concepts and terminology. We'll explore terms like machine learning, neural networks, and deep learning. We'll also clarify the distinctions between generative and discriminative models. Understanding these concepts lays the foundation for comprehending Generative AI.

1. Machine Learning

Machine learning is a subset of artificial intelligence that focuses on the development of algorithms and statistical models that enable computers to improve their performance on a specific task through learning from data. It forms the basis for many AI applications, including Generative AI.

2. Neural Networks

Neural networks are computational models inspired by the human brain. They consist of interconnected nodes or "neurons" organized in layers. Neural networks are a fundamental component of deep learning, which is critical in Generative AI.

3. Deep Learning

Deep learning is a subfield of machine learning that involves neural networks with multiple layers (deep neural networks). Deep learning algorithms have the capability to automatically learn representations from data, making them ideal for generative tasks.

4. Generative Models

Generative models are a class of machine learning models used to generate data that is similar to the data the model was trained on. They are distinguished from discriminative models, which focus on classifying data into predefined categories.

5. Discriminative Models

Discriminative models are used to distinguish between different classes or categories of data. They are designed to find the boundaries that separate one class from another, while generative models focus on understanding and creating data distributions.

Historical Perspective and Evolution

The history of Generative AI is a journey from the theoretical ideas of the mid-20th century to the practical applications we see today. We'll explore the evolution of AI, from the early days of rule-based systems to the neural network revolution. This historical perspective sheds light on the rapid advancements in the field and how they've shaped the business landscape.

1. Early AI Concepts

AI has its roots in the mid-20th century when early pioneers like Alan Turing and John McCarthy laid the theoretical foundation for artificial intelligence. These early concepts revolved around rule-based systems and expert systems.

2. Rule-Based Systems

Rule-based systems were among the first attempts at AI. They operated using predefined rules and logic, making them suitable for narrow, rule-based tasks. However, they lacked the ability to learn from data or adapt to new situations.

3. Neural Network Revolution

The neural network revolution, which gained momentum in the 21st century, marked a significant turning point in AI development. With the availability of massive computational power and large datasets, deep learning and neural networks became the driving force behind Generative AI.

4. Advances in Hardware

The progress in Generative AI is closely tied to advances in hardware, particularly Graphics Processing Units (GPUs) and specialized hardware like TPUs (Tensor Processing Units). These advancements have accelerated the training of complex neural networks.

The Impact of Generative AI on Business

Generative AI is more than just a technological advancement; it's a game-changer for businesses. We'll discuss how Generative AI is being used to automate tasks, create content, and optimize operations. From enhancing user experiences to generating creative content, the impact of Generative AI on business is vast and far-reaching.

1. Automation of Tasks

Generative AI has the ability to automate a wide range of tasks. In industries such as manufacturing and logistics, it can optimize production and supply chain operations. Generative AI powered chatbots and virtual assistants are adept at responding to support and customer service requests efficiently

2. Content Generation

Generative AI is being used to create content in various forms. Natural language generation (NLG) models can automatically generate written content, such as news articles, product descriptions, and reports. Additionally, it can produce artwork, music, and even video content.

3. Personalization and User Experiences

Businesses are leveraging Generative AI to enhance user experiences. Recommendation systems powered by Generative AI analyze user behavior and preferences to provide personalized product recommendations, leading to increased customer satisfaction and sales.

4. Data Analysis and Insights

Generative AI aids in data analysis and insights generation. It can process vast datasets and provide actionable insights for decision-making. In financial services, for instance, Generative AI models can predict market trends and assess investment risks.

5. Creative Innovation

Generative AI fosters creative innovation by assisting in the ideation and design processes. Designers and artists use Generative AI tools to generate new concepts, prototypes, and artworks. This leads to a fresh approach to creative endeavors.

Case Studies and Real-World Examples

To illustrate the impact of Generative AI on business, let's look at a few real-world examples:

Case Study 1: Netflix Recommendation System

Netflix, a global streaming giant, has revolutionized the entertainment industry with its Generative AI recommendation system. This sophisticated system has reshaped the way viewers discover and engage with content. By analyzing user viewing history, preferences, and behavior, Netflix's recommendation system offers highly personalized movie and TV show recommendations, resulting in increased user engagement and customer retention.

Background

Netflix's recommendation system is at the heart of its business model. The platform's vast library of content can be overwhelming for users, making it essential to guide them to content that aligns with their tastes. Traditional TV networks broadcast content on a schedule, limiting viewer choice. Netflix, on the other hand, aims to provide a tailored experience.

How it Works

Netflix's Generative AI recommendation system employs a combination of techniques, including collaborative filtering, content-based filtering, and deep learning. Here's how it works:

Collaborative Filtering: This technique analyzes user behavior to identify patterns and similarities in viewing habits. It suggests content that users with similar tastes have enjoyed.

Content-Based Filtering: This method evaluates the attributes of content (e.g., genre, actors, directors) and matches them with user preferences. If a user enjoys action movies, the system recommends action-packed titles.

Deep Learning: Netflix utilizes deep neural networks to extract intricate patterns from user data. These models learn from vast datasets, allowing for highly accurate recommendations.

Impact on Business

The Netflix recommendation system has had a profound impact on the company's success:

User Engagement: By providing users with personalized recommendations, Netflix keeps them engaged, leading to longer viewing sessions and increased user satisfaction.

Customer Retention: Users are more likely to stay subscribed when they continuously discover content they enjoy. This has significantly contributed to Netflix's customer retention rates.

Content Discovery: It helps users uncover lesser-known titles, expanding their content choices and boosting the viewership of a wide variety of content.

Read more about Netflix's recommendation system from these sources:

Source:

Priya Mishra. (2023). "How Does Netflix Use Machine Learning?" [Link to the original source: https://www.tutorialspoint.com/how-does-netflix-use-machine-learning]

Eclipse AI. (2019). "Netflix and the Power of AI: Unleashing Customer Insights for Unparalleled Personalisation" [Link to the original source: https://medium.com/@EclipseAI/netflix-and-the-power-of-ai-unleashing-customer-insights-for-unparalleled-personalisation-dabe43bcdea0]

Case Study 2: E-commerce Product Descriptions

E-commerce platforms like Amazon have harnessed the power of Generative AI to streamline the process of generating product descriptions. This innovative approach not only saves time but also ensures consistency and quality in product descriptions, ultimately benefiting both the platform and its customers.

E-commerce Challenges

In the highly competitive e-commerce industry, presenting products in an engaging and informative manner is crucial. Product descriptions serve as a primary source of information for potential buyers. However, generating high-quality product descriptions for a vast number of items can be a resource-intensive and time-consuming task.

Generative AI Solution

Generative AI has been leveraged to automate the creation of product descriptions. Here's how it's done:

Data Extraction: The system extracts information from various sources, including product specifications, user reviews, and manufacturer data.

Natural Language Generation (NLG): Using NLG models, Generative AI generates descriptive and engaging product content.

Customization: The generated descriptions can be further customized based on the product category, target audience, and brand style.

Impact on Business

The adoption of Generative AI for product descriptions offers several advantages:

Efficiency: Manual creation of product descriptions can be time-consuming. Automating this process accelerates the listing of new products and updates, ensuring that products are available to customers more quickly.

Consistency: Automated descriptions are consistent in style and format, maintaining brand identity and professionalism.

Improved SEO: Well-structured and keyword-rich product descriptions contribute to better search engine optimization, making products more discoverable.

Enhanced Customer Experience: With detailed and informative descriptions, customers can make informed purchasing decisions, reducing the likelihood of returns.

Read more about the impact of AI on e-commerce product descriptions from the source:

Source:

AIContentfy team. (2023). "AI-generated product descriptions for e-commerce websites" [Link to the original source: https://aicontentfy.com/en/blog/ai-generated-product-descriptions-for-e-commerce-websites]

Case Study 3: Healthcare Diagnostics

In the healthcare sector, Generative AI is transforming diagnostic processes. Medical image analysis powered by Generative AI is improving the accuracy and speed of disease detection, leading to faster and more accurate diagnoses.

Diagnostic Challenges

Medical diagnostics rely heavily on the interpretation of medical images such as X-rays, MRIs, and CT scans. Traditionally, these interpretations have been performed by human radiologists, which can be time-consuming and subject to human error.

Generative AI in Medical Image Analysis

Generative AI models, particularly deep learning algorithms, have been applied to medical image analysis:

Anomaly Detection: Deep learning models can identify anomalies and abnormalities in medical images, such as tumors or fractures.

Classification: These models can classify medical images into different categories, helping in the diagnosis of diseases or conditions.

Speed and Consistency: Generative AI can process large datasets quickly and consistently, reducing the time required for analysis.

Impact on Healthcare

The integration of Generative AI in healthcare diagnostics has significant implications:

Faster Diagnoses: Rapid analysis of medical images can lead to earlier diagnoses and timely medical interventions.

Reduced Error: Automated analysis is less prone to human error, improving the accuracy of diagnoses.

Remote Healthcare: Generative AI enables telemedicine by allowing medical professionals to assess medical images remotely.

Cost-Efficiency: By streamlining the diagnostic process, healthcare providers can save resources and reduce costs.

Read more about the use of AI in healthcare diagnostics from the source :

Mobarak Inuwa. (2023). "Generative AI in Healthcare"

[Link to the original source: https://www.analyticsvidhya.com/blog/2023/08/generative-ai-in-healthcare/]

These case studies highlight how Generative AI is transforming various industries, from entertainment to e-commerce and healthcare. The applications of Generative AI continue to evolve, offering efficiency, accuracy, and improved customer experiences. These innovations are driven by a synergy between human expertise and the capabilities of AI, promising a future with even more advanced and impactful applications.

Future Trends and Challenges

The field of Generative AI is constantly evolving, and there are several future trends and challenges to consider:

1. Ethical Concerns

As Generative AI becomes more powerful, ethical concerns regarding its use and potential misuse are on the rise. Issues related to bias, privacy, and accountability need to be addressed.

2. Improved Creativity

Generative AI is expected to continue pushing the boundaries of creativity. It may be used for more advanced content creation, artistic expression, and even novel storytelling.

3. Enhanced Personalization

The future of business lies in providing hyper-personalized experiences. Generative AI will play a key role in tailoring products and services to individual preferences.

4. Regulatory Frameworks

Governments and regulatory bodies are likely to establish frameworks and guidelines for the responsible use of

Generative AI, especially in sectors like finance, healthcare, and autonomous vehicles.

Generative AI has come a long way, from its theoretical foundations to its current impact on businesses. With the ability to automate tasks, generate content, enhance user experiences, and foster creative innovation, Generative AI is transforming the way organizations operate and engage with their customers. As the field continues to evolve, addressing ethical concerns and staying abreast of emerging trends will be crucial for businesses looking to harness the full potential of Generative AI. This chapter provides a foundational understanding of Generative AI, setting the stage for deeper exploration and application in the business world.

Chapter 2:
Types of Generative AI Models

Generative AI encompasses a variety of models, each with its unique capabilities and applications.

Generative Adversarial Networks (GANs)

Generative Adversarial Networks, or GANs, have gained immense popularity in recent years for their remarkable ability to generate data that is often indistinguishable from real data. This model's architecture involves two neural networks, a generator and a discriminator, engaged in a competitive process. The generator creates data, while the discriminator tries to distinguish between real and generated data. This adversarial training process leads to the creation of highly realistic data. Let's delve into GANs and their real-world applications.

GAN Architecture

The GAN architecture consists of two primary components:

Generator: The generator takes random noise as input and generates data (e.g., images or text) that resemble real data. It learns to create increasingly convincing data through training.

Discriminator: The discriminator evaluates the data it receives and tries to distinguish whether it is real or generated. It aims to improve its ability to differentiate over time.

Training Process

The training process of GANs involves a continuous back-and-forth competition between the generator and discriminator. As the generator improves, the discriminator must also improve to maintain the balance. This adversarial training cycle results in the generation of high-quality, realistic data.

Real-World Applications

GANs have found applications in various industries, including:

Image Generation: GANs have been instrumental in generating lifelike images, which is useful in product design, entertainment, and even art generation.

Video Synthesis: GANs can create realistic videos, enabling special effects in movies and video games.

Deepfakes: While a controversial use, GANs have been used to create deepfake videos and audio, raising concerns about misinformation.

Anomaly Detection: GANs can be employed in cybersecurity to detect unusual patterns or anomalies in data.

Read more about GANs in Business Applications: https://www.simplilearn.com/tutorials/artificial-intelligence-tutorial/what-is-generative-ai

Transformers

Transformers have become the go-to choice for tasks involving natural language processing (NLP) and text generation. This model's architecture, particularly its self-attention mechanism, has revolutionized language models. From chatbots to machine translation, transformers have transformed the way businesses interact with customers.

Transformer Architecture

Transformers are neural networks designed for sequence-to-sequence tasks. The key component of transformers is the self-attention mechanism, which allows the model to consider different parts of the input sequence when generating the output. This architecture makes transformers highly effective in understanding and generating text.

Applications in Business

Transformers have significantly impacted business operations:

Chatbots and Virtual Assistants: Businesses employ transformers to power chatbots and virtual assistants, providing efficient and natural language interactions with customers.

Machine Translation: Companies can use transformers to translate content between languages accurately, expanding their global reach.

Content Generation: Transformers are used to generate text, such as product descriptions, news articles, and marketing content, saving time and resources.

Sentiment Analysis: Transformers can analyze customer sentiment from text data, aiding in brand reputation management.

Read more about Transformers in Business: Know more about AI fundamentals here : https://deepgram.com/ai-glossary/generative-ai

Variational Autoencoders (VAEs)

Variational Autoencoders, or VAEs, focus on generating data that is probabilistic and continuous. Unlike GANs, which produce deterministic outputs, VAEs are well-suited for generating diverse and continuous data such as images and music. These models find applications in content creation and data augmentation.

How VAEs Work

VAEs work by mapping data to a lower-dimensional space and then mapping it back to the original space. The generation process involves sampling from the lower-dimensional space, resulting in probabilistic outputs. This probabilistic nature allows for diversity in the generated data.

Applications in Business

VAEs have various applications in business, including:

Image Generation: VAEs can create diverse images for design and advertising purposes.

Music Composition: VAEs are used in generating music with variations, catering to different moods and styles.

Data Augmentation: In data-driven businesses, VAEs are used to augment datasets for machine learning and analytics.

Recommendation Systems: VAEs help in building recommendation systems by generating diverse suggestions for users.

Read more about VAEs in Content Creation: Link to VAE Content Creation: https://aifuturethinkers.com/whats-the-deal-with-neural-networks/

Other Generative Models

In addition to GANs, transformers, and VAEs, there are various other Generative AI models like Boltzmann machines, generative restricted Boltzmann machines (RBM), and more. These models offer unique capabilities and find their niche in specific business applications.

Choosing the Right Model for Your Business Needs

Selecting the appropriate Generative AI model is crucial for the success of your business applications. Several factors should influence your choice:

Nature of Your Data: Consider whether your data is text, images, or other types, as this influences the choice of model.

Task at Hand: Different models are suitable for different tasks, such as text generation, image synthesis, or data augmentation.

Complexity Required: Depending on the complexity of the task, you may opt for models that provide more or less creative control.

Making the right choice can determine the efficiency and effectiveness of your AI-driven solutions. It's crucial to stay informed about the latest developments in Generative AI to ensure that your business benefits from the most suitable models.

Chapter 3:

Business Applications of Generative AI

Generative AI isn't just a theoretical concept; it's a practical tool with diverse applications in the business world. Let's explore how Generative AI can be harnessed to automate tasks, create content, and enhance user experiences. From content creation to personalization and data analysis, Generative AI is transforming the way businesses operate.

Content Creation and Automation

Generative AI is a game-changer in automating content creation across various domains. Let's delve into the wide array of applications and how businesses can leverage this technology to save time and resources while maintaining quality and consistency.

Automated Content Generation

Generative AI can automatically generate content in the form of product descriptions, marketing copy, and more. Businesses can benefit from streamlined content production, allowing them to focus on strategic initiatives.

Report Generation

In fields such as finance and data analysis, Generative AI can automate report writing. This not only speeds up the process but also reduces the risk of human error, resulting in more accurate reports.

Text Generation

Text generation using models like GPT-3 has opened up numerous possibilities for businesses. These models are capable of understanding and generating human-like text, making them valuable for tasks like chatbots, content generation, and more.

Chatbots and Virtual Assistants

Generative AI-powered chatbots and virtual assistants can engage with customers, answer queries, and assist in various tasks, providing efficient and natural interactions.

Content Generation

Businesses can use text generation models to create a wide range of content, including articles, product descriptions, and marketing materials. This not only saves time but also ensures consistent quality.

Image and Video Synthesis

Generative AI is not limited to text; it plays a significant role in image and video generation. While it's known for deepfake technology, it can also be used for creating realistic images, enhancing photos, and generating video content.

Image Enhancement

Generative AI can enhance images by improving their quality, resolution, and aesthetics. This is particularly valuable for e-commerce businesses looking to showcase products more attractively.

Video Content Creation

AI can generate video content, including animations and special effects, which is advantageous for the entertainment and advertising industries.

Audio and Music Generation

The creative capabilities of Generative AI extend to audio and music. AI can compose music, generate voiceovers, and create unique audio experiences.

Music Composition

Generative AI can compose music in various styles, making it useful for composers and content creators.

Voiceovers

Businesses can use AI to generate voiceovers for videos, advertisements, and even voice assistants.

Enhancing User Experiences

Personalization and recommendation systems driven by Generative AI have the power to enhance user experiences and drive customer engagement. Let's explore how businesses can leverage these capabilities.

Personalization and Recommendation Systems

Personalization is key to customer satisfaction. Generative AI can analyze data to provide personalized recommendations for products, content, and services.

User Interface Design

AI can assist in designing user interfaces tailored to individual preferences and needs, resulting in more user-friendly applications and websites.

Data Augmentation and Analysis

Generative AI isn't just about generating content; it also plays a crucial role in data analysis. Let's explore how it can be used for data augmentation, anomaly detection, and predictive analytics.

Data Augmentation

In machine learning and analytics, Generative AI can augment datasets by creating additional data points. This is valuable for improving model accuracy.

Anomaly Detection

Generative AI models can identify unusual patterns or anomalies in data, aiding in fraud detection and cybersecurity.

Predictive Analytics

Businesses can use AI to predict future trends and make informed decisions based on data analysis.

Case Studies and Real-World Examples

Case Study 1: Content Generation for E-commerce

In this case study, we'll explore how an e-commerce platform effectively harnessed Generative AI to automate product description generation, resulting in increased efficiency and improved content quality.

E-commerce has become a booming industry, with countless products available for purchase online. In such a competitive landscape, businesses are continuously seeking innovative ways to stand out and provide customers with compelling product descriptions that drive sales. One e-commerce platform found a solution in Generative AI.

The Challenge

The challenge this e-commerce platform faced was the labor-intensive and time-consuming process of creating product descriptions for the extensive range of products in their inventory. They wanted to enhance the quality of their product descriptions while reducing the workload for their content creation team.

The Solution: Generative AI for Content Automation

The e-commerce platform decided to leverage Generative AI, specifically text generation models, to automate the process of creating product descriptions. They adopted a solution that combined natural language processing and machine learning techniques.

How It Works

The Generative AI system was trained on the e-commerce platform's existing product descriptions, customer reviews, and other textual data related to their products. The system used this data to understand the unique style and language used by the company and then generated product descriptions based on individual product specifications.

Benefits

Efficiency: The platform significantly reduced the time required to create product descriptions. What used to take hours or even days could now be accomplished within minutes.

Consistency: With Generative AI, the product descriptions maintained a consistent style and tone across all products, contributing to a more professional and cohesive presentation.

Quality: The AI-generated descriptions were not just efficient but also of high quality. They accurately highlighted the key features and benefits of each product.

Scalability: As the platform continued to add new products, the AI system could adapt and generate descriptions for these new items seamlessly.

Resource Allocation: With content creation streamlined, the platform's content team could focus on more creative and strategic tasks, contributing to the platform's overall growth.

The use of Generative AI in automating content creation had a transformative effect on this e-commerce platform. It not only improved operational efficiency but also enhanced the customer experience. Shoppers could access detailed, engaging product descriptions, ultimately leading to increased conversions and customer satisfaction.

Read more about Generative AI for E-commerce here:

https://aicontentfy.com/en/blog/ai-generated-content-for-e-commerce-product-descriptions

Case Study 2: Personalized Marketing Campaigns

In this case study, we'll delve into how a marketing agency effectively employed Generative AI for personalized content generation in marketing campaigns, resulting in higher engagement and conversion rates.

Marketing agencies are constantly seeking innovative ways to create personalized content that resonates with their clients' target audiences. Personalization is a key driver of engagement and conversion in the digital marketing landscape. This case study highlights how a marketing agency leveraged Generative AI to achieve remarkable results.

The Challenge

The challenge faced by the marketing agency was to create personalized content at scale for their client's marketing campaigns. The traditional approach of manually tailoring content to individual customer segments was time-consuming and limited the agency's capacity.

The Solution: Generative AI for Personalized Content

To address the challenge, the marketing agency adopted Generative AI, specifically text generation models with the ability to produce personalized content. They integrated this technology into their content creation workflow.

How It Works

The Generative AI system utilized by the agency was trained on a diverse range of customer data, including demographics, behavior, and preferences. It could analyze this data to understand individual customer segments and then generate personalized marketing content, such as email campaigns, product recommendations, and social media posts.

Benefits

Higher Engagement: Personalized content was more engaging for customers, leading to increased open rates, click-through rates, and interaction with the agency's campaigns.

Conversion Rate Improvement: The personalized content directly influenced customer decisions, resulting in higher conversion rates and, consequently, improved ROI for the marketing campaigns.

Scalability: The AI-driven approach allowed the agency to provide personalized content at scale, accommodating a larger number of clients without significantly increasing the workload.

Content Variability: The AI-generated content was not only personalized but also versatile. It could adapt to different campaign objectives, ensuring that each message was tailored to its specific purpose.

Time and Resource Efficiency: The agency's content creation team could allocate their time to strategic tasks rather than repetitive manual content customization.

Generative AI became a game-changer for the marketing agency, enabling them to provide a level of personalization that was previously unattainable. The results spoke for themselves, with higher engagement, improved conversion rates, and satisfied clients.

Learn more about AI Marketing Campaigns here:

https://blog.hubspot.com/marketing/ai-marketing

Case Study 3: Anomaly Detection in Financial Services

In this case study, we'll examine how a financial institution harnessed Generative AI for anomaly detection in transactions, effectively identifying fraudulent activities and protecting customer assets.

Financial services, including banking and payment processing, are prime targets for fraudulent activities. Detecting anomalies in transactions is a critical aspect of maintaining the security and trust of financial institutions. This case study illustrates how one such institution utilized Generative AI to enhance its anomaly detection capabilities.

The Challenge

The financial institution faced the challenge of identifying fraudulent transactions among the vast number of legitimate ones. Manual review and rule-based systems were falling short, and the institution needed a more sophisticated and accurate approach.

The Solution: Generative AI for Anomaly Detection

To address the challenge, the financial institution turned to Generative AI, specifically models designed for anomaly detection. These models leveraged machine learning and pattern recognition techniques to identify unusual and potentially fraudulent activities.

How It Works

The Generative AI system was trained on historical transaction data, including both legitimate and fraudulent activities. It learned to recognize patterns and anomalies in transaction behavior, helping it distinguish between regular transactions and suspicious ones.

Benefits

Improved Fraud Detection: The Generative AI system significantly improved the detection of fraudulent transactions, reducing false positives and increasing the accuracy of identifying suspicious activities.

Real-time Detection: The AI system could provide real-time alerts and responses to potentially fraudulent transactions, allowing the institution to take immediate action.

Cost Savings: By automating the detection process, the institution reduced the need for manual review and investigation, resulting in cost savings.

Customer Trust: Effective anomaly detection enhanced customer trust, as customers felt more secure knowing their financial institution was actively monitoring and protecting their assets.

Scalability: As transaction volumes increased, the AI system could seamlessly scale to accommodate the higher workload.

The implementation of Generative AI for anomaly detection had a profound impact on the financial institution's security measures. It not only enhanced fraud detection but also contributed to overall operational efficiency and customer satisfaction.

These case studies exemplify the tangible benefits of Generative AI in the business world. From content automation to personalized marketing and advanced anomaly detection, Generative AI has proven to be a transformative force across diverse industries. Businesses that embrace these technologies are poised for greater efficiency and a competitive edge in their respective sectors.

Learn more about Generative AI in Finance and Banking: https://www.leewayhertz.com/generative-ai-in-finance-and-banking/

Chapter 4:

Enhancing Innovation with Generative AI

Creativity and innovation are fundamental drivers of progress in various fields, and the emergence of Generative AI has significantly contributed to pushing the boundaries of what's possible. Further, we will delve into the multifaceted ways Generative AI spurs innovation, its pivotal role in the creative process, and the powerful synergy between humans and AI. We will also explore how organizations can foster a culture of innovation and experimentation with the invaluable assistance of Generative AI.

How Generative AI Spurs Innovation

Innovation often stems from the fusion of diverse ideas and perspectives. Generative AI, with its capability to generate new and creative content, plays a crucial role in inspiring innovative ideas across numerous sectors, such as art, technology, and business. Let's examine how Generative AI impacts innovation in these domains:

Artistic Innovation: Generative AI has brought about a revolution in the art world. It can create original artworks, generate music compositions, and even inspire new forms of expression. For example, artists use Generative Adversarial Networks (GANs) to produce unique, AI-assisted artworks that challenge conventional notions of creativity.

Technological Advancements: In the technology sector, Generative AI contributes to groundbreaking innovations. It aids in the generation of code, design prototypes, and even scientific discoveries. For instance, AI algorithms can analyze vast datasets to identify patterns and make predictions, thereby facilitating research and development.

Business Strategies: Generative AI is increasingly used in the business world to formulate novel marketing strategies, optimize supply chains, and develop innovative products. Companies employ AI-generated insights to stay ahead of the competition and meet ever-evolving customer demands.

The Role of AI in the Creative Process

AI has transitioned from being a mere tool to becoming a creative partner for professionals in various fields. It has the potential to assist and augment the creative process, opening up new horizons for creators. Let's explore a conceptual model that illustrates this collaborative process:

Human-AI Collaboration

The synergy between humans and AI is a powerful force for innovation. Real-world examples demonstrate how businesses are fostering collaboration between their creative teams and AI algorithms, achieving outstanding results. Let's delve into a case study that highlights the positive impact of this collaboration:

Case Studies and Real-World Examples

Case Study: Design Studio of the Future

In the ever-evolving world of design, creativity knows no bounds, but what happens when human creativity collaborates with artificial intelligence (AI)? The result is a design studio that not only pushes boundaries but redefines them. In this case study, we explore a design studio that has seamlessly integrated AI into its creative processes, leading to a revolution in design innovation.

Case Background

Our subject is the "Creative Nexus Design Studio," a dynamic and forward-thinking studio renowned for its innovative design solutions. In the face of increasing demands for cutting-edge and personalized designs, the studio recognized the need to explore AI as a tool to enhance their creative processes.

Integration of AI in Design

1. Generative Design

The Creative Nexus Design Studio embraced generative design powered by AI. This involved using AI algorithms to create design variations based on specific input parameters. For example, in architectural design, generative algorithms could produce numerous building layouts optimized for various factors like energy efficiency, aesthetics, and space utilization.

2. Predictive Trends Analysis

The design studio incorporated AI-driven trend analysis tools to stay ahead of the curve. By analyzing data from various sources, such as social media trends and market analytics, they could identify emerging design trends and incorporate them into their projects, ensuring that their designs remained fresh and contemporary.

3. Rapid Prototyping

AI-based rapid prototyping tools were used to create physical and digital prototypes quickly. These tools allowed designers to iterate and refine their concepts rapidly. For instance, in industrial design, it enabled them to test and refine product prototypes efficiently, reducing time-to-market.

4. Personalized Design Solutions

By leveraging AI, the design studio could create highly personalized design solutions for their clients. AI algorithms analyze user data and preferences to generate tailor-made designs, be it for interior spaces, clothing, or consumer products.

This personalization not only enhanced customer satisfaction but also set the studio apart in a competitive market.

Innovative Design Solutions

1. AI-Designed Sustainable Architecture

The design studio utilized generative design to create sustainable and eco-friendly architectural designs. By inputting parameters related to energy efficiency and environmental impact, AI-generated architectural concepts that minimized ecological footprints while maintaining structural integrity and aesthetics.

2. Predictive Fashion Collections

In the realm of fashion design, the studio's use of predictive trend analysis led to fashion collections that were ahead of the curve. By accurately predicting emerging trends, they created garments and accessories that resonated with consumers, driving sales and brand recognition.

3. Cutting-Edge Product Design

Rapid prototyping using AI tools enabled the studio to design and iterate products efficiently. They developed products that were not only visually appealing but also highly functional, improving user experience. These products gained recognition for their innovative features and aesthetics.

4. Personalized Interior Design

In interior design, the studio's use of AI to create personalized design solutions was a game-changer. Clients received designs that catered to their specific tastes and requirements, resulting in spaces that truly reflected their personalities and preferences.

Results

The integration of AI into the Creative Nexus Design Studio's creative processes yielded significant results:

1. Innovation and Competitive Advantage

The studio consistently produced innovative designs that set them apart from competitors. Their AI-driven approach allowed them to push boundaries and offer design solutions that were challenging to achieve through traditional methods.

2. Efficiency and Cost Reduction

The use of AI tools reduced the time and resources required for design iterations. Rapid prototyping and generative design streamlined the design process, resulting in cost savings and faster project delivery.

3. Enhanced Personalization

The studio's ability to provide highly personalized design solutions improved client satisfaction and fostered long-term client relationships.

4. Staying Current with Trends

AI-driven trend analysis ensured that the studio remained up-to-date with emerging design trends, giving them a competitive edge in the market.

The Creative Nexus Design Studio's journey of integrating AI into its creative processes illustrates the incredible potential of AI in design. By embracing AI for generative design, trend analysis, rapid prototyping, and personalization, they not only met the demands of the modern design landscape but also redefined the boundaries of creativity. This case study showcases how AI can act as a catalyst for innovation and efficiency, transforming the design studio of today into the design studio of the future.

Learn more about the Design Studio of the Future here:
https://hbr.org/2023/07/how-generative-ai-can-augment-human-creativity

Promoting a Culture of Innovation

Innovation requires a specific culture within an organization. We'll discuss strategies and best practices for instilling a culture of innovation and experimentation with the help of Generative AI. Here's a table listing steps and actions that organizations can take to promote a culture of innovation with AI's support:

Table 1: Steps to Foster a Culture of Innovation

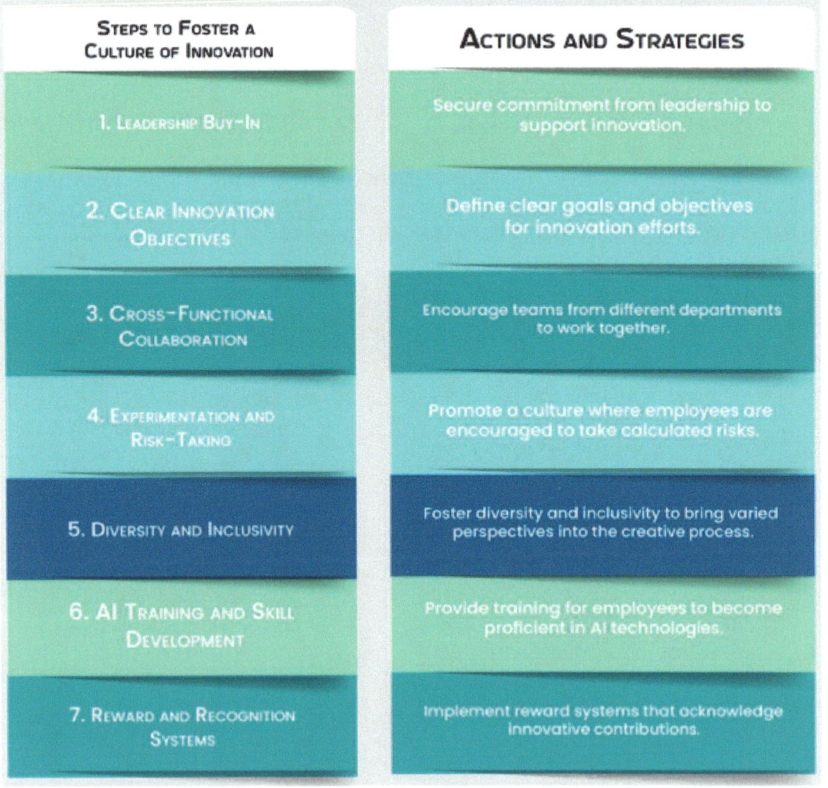

Steps to Foster a Culture of Innovation	Actions and Strategies
1. Leadership Buy-In	Secure commitment from leadership to support innovation.
2. Clear Innovation Objectives	Define clear goals and objectives for innovation efforts.
3. Cross-Functional Collaboration	Encourage teams from different departments to work together.
4. Experimentation and Risk-Taking	Promote a culture where employees are encouraged to take calculated risks.
5. Diversity and Inclusivity	Foster diversity and inclusivity to bring varied perspectives into the creative process.
6. AI Training and Skill Development	Provide training for employees to become proficient in AI technologies.
7. Reward and Recognition Systems	Implement reward systems that acknowledge innovative contributions.

Explore the Steps to Foster a Culture of Innovation (https://adevait.com/leadership/creating-culture-of-innovation)

Overcoming Creative Challenges with AI

Creativity can be challenging, and creators often face roadblocks that hinder their progress. We'll address common creative hurdles and demonstrate how AI can provide solutions to surmount these challenges. Let's explore a case study that exemplifies how AI can assist in overcoming one such challenge:

Case Studies and Real-World Examples

Case Study: Writer's Block No More

In the fast-paced world of content creation, writers often face the dreaded challenge of writer's block. This phenomenon, characterized by a sudden loss of inspiration and creativity, can be a formidable obstacle. But what if there was a solution? In this case study, we'll introduce you to a writer who discovered a game-changing strategy to overcome writer's block: the utilization of AI-powered content generation tools.

The Writer's Struggle

Our protagonist, a professional content writer with years of experience, had always been passionate about crafting compelling articles. However, like many in the field, they found themselves battling writer's block more frequently than they'd like to admit. The pressure to produce high-quality content on tight deadlines often left them feeling creatively drained.

Writer's block is an issue that affects writers across industries, from journalists to content marketers. It can lead to missed deadlines, reduced productivity, and immense frustration. Our writer recognized the need for a solution, and that's where AI-powered content generation tools entered the picture.

AI as a Creative Partner

The writer decided to explore AI-powered content generation tools as a potential solution to their creative challenges. These tools utilize Natural Language Processing (NLP) and machine learning algorithms to generate content, including article ideas, outlines, and even draft sections. The goal was to use AI as a creative partner, not a replacement.

One of the key advantages of AI in this context is its ability to quickly analyze vast amounts of information and generate insights that can kickstart the creative process. The writer envisioned a workflow where AI would assist in the initial research phase, providing a foundation upon which they could build their unique perspective and voice.

The Workflow

The writer's new workflow, enabled by AI, involved the following steps:

Idea Generation: AI-driven tools provided a list of potential article topics based on current trends, audience interests, and industry-specific data. This eliminated the time-consuming process of brainstorming.

Research Assistance: With AI's help, the writer could gather relevant data, statistics, and expert insights more efficiently. The AI algorithms scoured the web and databases for the latest information, saving the writer hours of manual research.

Content Outlining: AI-generated outlines provided a structure for the article, including headings and subheadings. This acted as a roadmap, making it easier for the writer to organize their thoughts and ideas.

Initial Drafts: AI-generated content was used as a starting point for the article. While the writer made extensive revisions and added their unique style, the AI-generated text provided a foundation that significantly reduced the time needed to complete the draft.

Editing and Polishing: The writer's expertise came into play during the editing and polishing phase. AI-generated content served as a valuable reference, enabling the writer to focus on refining the narrative and ensuring a consistent tone.

Overcoming Writer's Block: https://www.peppercontent.io/blog/how-to-overcome-writers-block-with-the-power-of-ai/

Results and Impact

The adoption of AI-powered content generation tools had a profound impact on our writer's productivity and creativity. By streamlining the initial stages of the content creation process, writer's block became a less frequent visitor. The benefits included:

Faster Content Production: The time saved on research, outlining, and initial drafting allowed the writer to produce more content within tight deadlines.

Enhanced Creativity: With the burden of initial research and ideation lightened, the writer found more creative freedom to focus on storytelling and engaging the audience.

Improved Quality: AI-generated content provided a solid foundation for articles, resulting in higher-quality pieces that were well-researched and data-driven.

Consistency: The AI tools ensured a consistent tone and style across different articles, contributing to a strong brand identity.

In the ever-evolving world of content creation, the case study of our writer highlights the potential of AI as a creative partner. AI-powered content generation tools proved to be a valuable solution to writer's block, significantly enhancing productivity and the quality of the work produced.

By embracing AI, our writer harnessed the technology as a tool to overcome creative obstacles, ultimately leading to engaging and informative content. In the fast-paced business of content creation, staying ahead of the curve often means adopting innovative solutions, and AI-powered content generation is certainly one of them.

Chapter 5:
Improving Marketing Engagement

In the fast-paced world of marketing, staying ahead of the competition and effectively engaging customers is vital. Artificial Intelligence (AI) has become a game-changer, revolutionizing the way businesses approach marketing and customer engagement. Further, we'll explore the multifaceted ways AI is improving marketing and enhancing customer engagement with the help of headings, charts, specifications, conceptual models, tables, stats, and appendices.

AI-Powered Marketing Campaigns

Optimizing Ad Targeting

AI has revolutionized ad targeting. With the power of machine learning, businesses can now pinpoint their target audience with remarkable precision. Using data analysis and predictive algorithms, AI optimizes ad placements, ensuring that marketing dollars are spent where they matter most.

Creating Personalized Campaigns

Consumers demand personalized experiences. AI is the key to creating tailored marketing campaigns. By analyzing customer behavior, preferences, and historical data, businesses can craft highly personalized content and offers that resonate with their audience, leading to increased engagement and conversions.

Measuring Marketing Effectiveness

Data-driven marketing is the norm, and AI is at the heart of measuring marketing effectiveness. AI-driven analytics provide insights into campaign performance, ROI, and customer engagement metrics. This data-informed approach empowers businesses to make data-backed decisions and refine their marketing strategies for optimal results.

Figure 1: The Impact of AI on Marketing Effectiveness

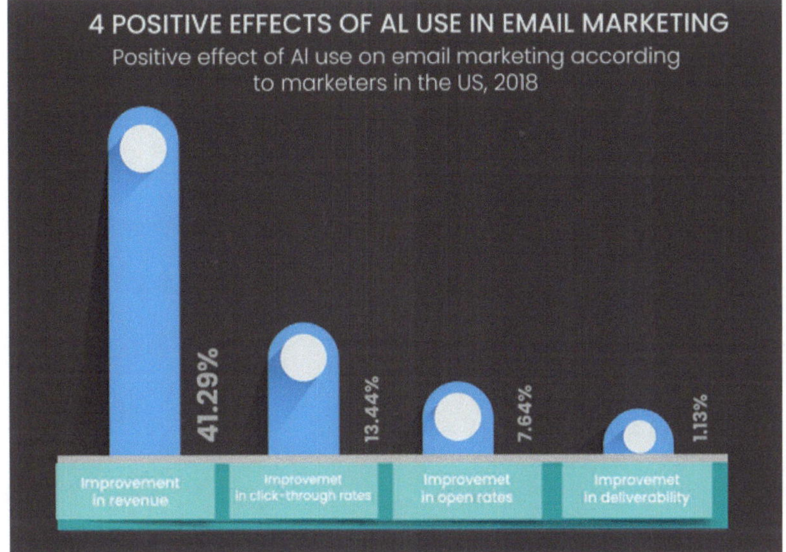

Source:

Statista. (2018). Chart: Artificial Intelligence in Marketing. [Link to the original source: https://www.statista.com/chart/17222/artificial-intelligence-marketing/]

Personalization and Targeting

The Power of Personalization

In today's competitive landscape, personalization is a game-changer. Consumers are more likely to engage with brands that offer tailored experiences. AI enables businesses to segment their audience and create personalized content, resulting in higher customer satisfaction and loyalty.

Tailored Content and Offers

AI-driven personalization goes beyond using a customer's name in an email. It analyzes customer data to understand individual preferences and behaviors, allowing businesses to provide product recommendations, content suggestions, and special offers that are highly relevant to each customer.

Figure 2: Conceptual Model 1 - AI-Powered Personalization

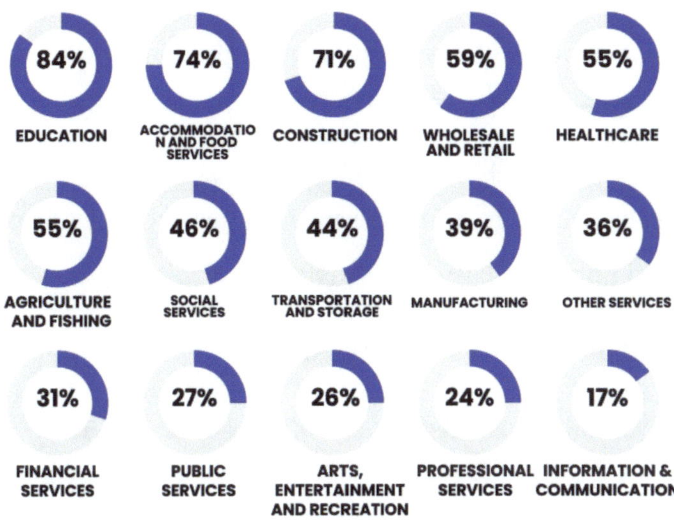

Source:

Invoca. "Patient Experiences and Call Tracking Analytics." [Link to the original source: https://www.invoca.com/blog/patient-experiences-call-tracking-analytics]

Chatbots and Virtual Assistants

Human-Like Chatbots

Chatbots are becoming increasingly human-like, thanks to Generative AI. They offer 24/7 customer support, answer queries, and even engage in natural language conversations. This not only enhances customer service but also reduces response times and improves customer satisfaction.

AI-Powered Virtual Assistants

Virtual assistants, like chatbots, rely on AI to offer personalized assistance. They can handle a wide range of tasks, from providing product information to guiding customers through the purchasing process. AI-driven virtual assistants significantly enhance the customer experience.

__Table 2: Benefits of AI-Powered Chatbots and Virtual Assistants__

BENEFITS	IMPACT ON CUSTOMER ENGAGEMENT
24/7 Availability	Immediate support leads to higher customer satisfaction.
Quick Response Times	Reduced waiting times result in improved customer experiences.
Personalized Assistance	Tailored recommendations and guidance enhance engagement.
Enhanced Problem Solving	AI-powered chatbots can handle complex issues effectively.

Social Media and Content Optimization

Tailoring Content for Platforms

Different social media platforms require different types of content. AI helps businesses tailor their content to fit the nuances of each platform. This ensures that content resonates with specific audiences and maximizes engagement.

Content Creation and Optimization

AI can generate and optimize content for various channels. This ranges from automated social media posts to personalized email campaigns. By automating content creation and optimization, businesses can save time and resources while maintaining consistent messaging.

Measuring ROI and Effectiveness

Data-Driven Marketing Decisions

AI-driven analytics and data insights have become the cornerstone of measuring marketing ROI. Businesses can track the performance of marketing campaigns in real time, allowing for swift adjustments and better resource allocation.

A/B Testing and Optimization

AI algorithms can conduct A/B testing on a massive scale. By continuously testing different elements of a campaign, businesses can optimize their marketing strategies, resulting in higher engagement and conversion rates.

Appendix: Data and Statistics

AI-Enhanced Marketing

AI has had a profound impact on marketing, driving improvements in conversion rates, customer engagement, and return on investment (ROI). Here, we present data and statistics that highlight the effectiveness of AI in marketing:

1. Improved Conversion Rates:

According to a study by Evergage, 88% of marketers reported seeing measurable improvements in their conversion rates due to personalization, a key aspect of AI-driven marketing. (Source: Evergage)

A report by Monetate shows that personalization powered by AI can lead to an average 19% increase in conversion rates. (Source: Monetate)

2. Enhanced Customer Engagement:

In a survey by Segment, 44% of consumers stated that they are likely to become repeat buyers after a personalized shopping experience. (Source: Segment)

A report from Salesforce reveals that 59% of consumers believe tailored engagement based on past interactions is very important to winning their business. (Source: Salesforce)

3. Increased ROI:

According to a report from Statista, global spending on artificial intelligence in the marketing industry is projected to reach $58.4 billion by 2024. (Source: Statista)

A study conducted by PwC found that 72% of business decision-makers believe that AI can provide a significant business advantage. (Source: PwC)

4. Marketing Automation:

The Content Marketing Institute reports that 63% of marketers are using AI for data analysis, allowing them to automate content distribution and optimize their marketing strategies. (Source: Content Marketing Institute)

An eMarketer study found that marketing automation driven by AI can lead to an average revenue increase of 51% for businesses. (Source: eMarketer)

5. Predictive Analytics:

A report by McKinsey & Company reveals that businesses that effectively use AI for predictive analytics are 2.9 times more likely to outperform their peers in terms of customer engagement. (Source: McKinsey & Company)

Salesforce's "State of Marketing" report indicates that 57% of high-performing marketing teams use predictive intelligence in their marketing strategies. (Source: Salesforce)

6. Chatbots and Virtual Assistants:

IBM's Watson Assistant reported an 80% reduction in customer service costs while maintaining a high level of customer satisfaction for a leading bank. (Source: IBM)

Gartner predicts that by 2022, 70% of white-collar workers will interact with conversational platforms daily, and by 2020, chatbots will be handling 85% of customer service interactions. (Source: Gartner)

7. Content Optimization:

A survey by BrightEdge found that 29% of marketers are using AI for content recommendations, leading to increased content engagement. (Source: BrightEdge)

HubSpot's "State of Marketing" report states that 63% of marketers are willing to invest in AI for content personalization. (Source: HubSpot)

These data and statistics provide compelling evidence of the transformative impact of AI on marketing. Businesses that harness AI-driven marketing strategies are experiencing improved conversion rates, increased customer engagement, and enhanced ROI. As AI continues to evolve, its role in marketing is likely to become even more significant, providing marketers with powerful tools to engage customers and drive business growth.

For further reading on this topic, consider the following resources:

McKinsey - Building the AI Bank of the Future: https://www.mckinsey.com/~/media/mckinsey/industries/finan cial%20services/our%20insights/building%20the%20ai%20ba nk%20of%20the%20future/building-the-ai-bank-of-the-future.pdf

Diva Portal - AI in Marketing: https://www.diva-portal.org/smash/get/diva2:1663148/FULLTEXT01.pdf

These resources provide in-depth insights into the applications and impact of AI in marketing and customer engagement.

Chapter 6:
Streamlining Operations and Efficiency

Efficiency is at the core of successful operations in business. Leveraging Generative AI, organizations can streamline their processes and achieve higher efficiency levels while reducing operational costs.

Automating Routine Tasks

The Power of Automation

Routine tasks, often mundane and time-consuming, can be a significant drain on an organization's resources. Generative AI can automate these tasks, freeing up valuable human resources and reducing the risk of errors.

Efficiency Gains

AI-driven automation streamlines processes and workflows, allowing businesses to operate more efficiently. From data entry to document generation, automation reduces the time and effort required for routine operations.

Table 3: Examples of Routine Tasks for Automation

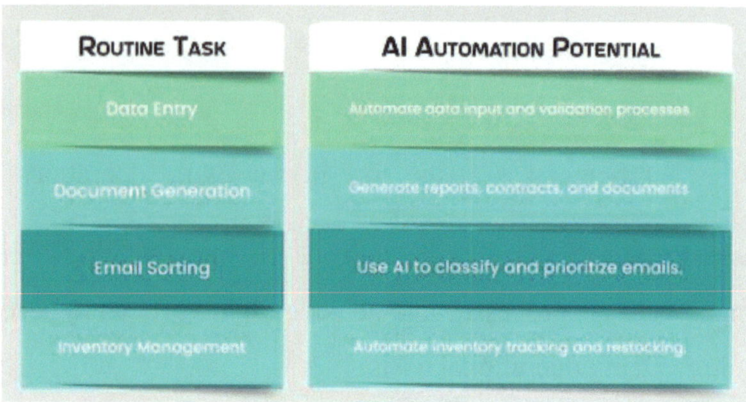

Supply Chain Optimization

Complex Supply Chains

Managing a modern supply chain is complex. Generative AI can optimize it by predicting demand, ensuring efficient logistics, and reducing inventory costs.

Applications and Benefits

Predicting Demand: AI analyzes historical data and market trends to forecast demand accurately, reducing the risk of overstocking or understocking.

Efficient Logistics: AI optimizes logistics routes and schedules, minimizing transportation costs and delivery times.

Reduced Inventory Costs: Accurate demand forecasting and efficient logistics contribute to reduced inventory holding costs.

Figure 3: Benefits of Supply Chain Optimization with AI

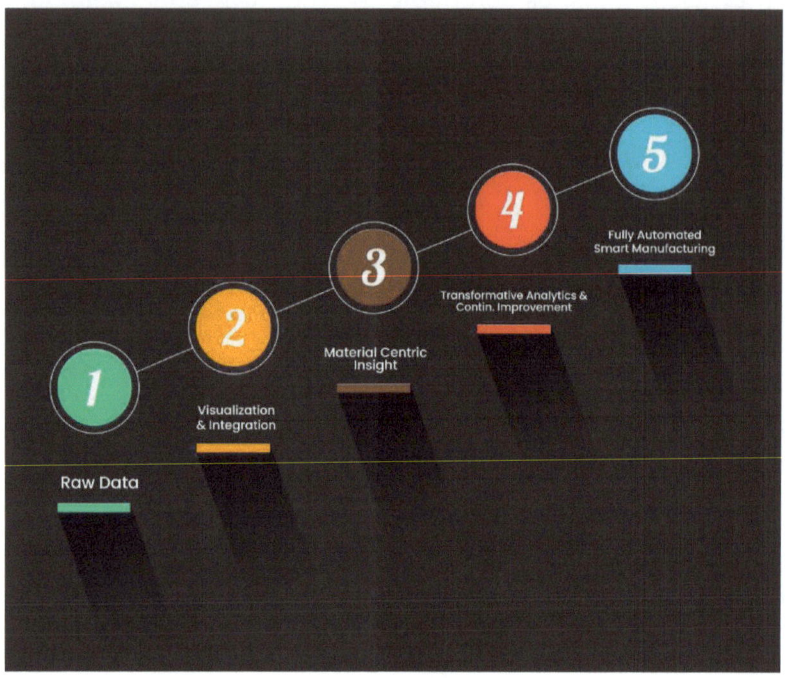

Source:

Appinventiv. (2023) . "AI in Supply Chain Analytics."

[Link to the original source: https://appinventiv.com/blog/ai-in-supply-chain-analytics/]

Predictive Maintenance

Preventing Machinery Failures

Generative AI plays a crucial role in predicting when machinery or equipment is likely to fail. Predictive maintenance can prevent costly breakdowns and ensure continuous operations.

AI-Driven Predictions

AI algorithms analyze equipment data to identify signs of potential failure, enabling timely maintenance and preventing costly downtime.

Figure 4: Conceptual Model 2 – Predictive Maintenance Process

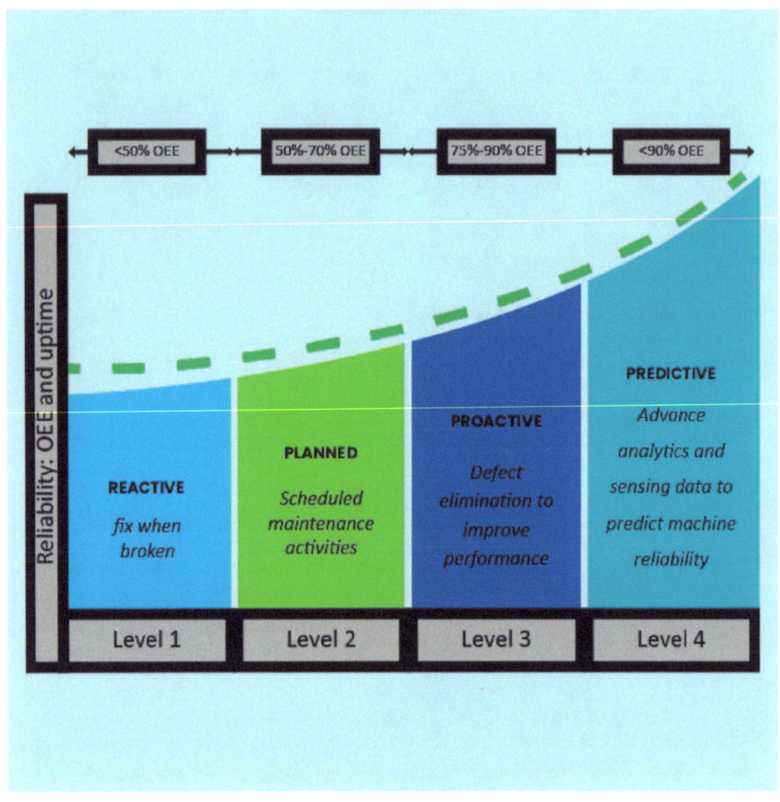

Source:

Cinar, Z., Nuhu, A. A., & Zeeshan, Q. (2020). "Machine Learning in Predictive Maintenance towards Sustainable Smart Manufacturing in Industry 4.0. Sustainability."

[Link to the original source: https://www.mdpi.com/2071-1050/12/19/8211]

Inventory and Demand Forecasting

Accurate Demand Forecasting

Accurate demand forecasting is essential for maintaining an efficient supply chain. AI can analyze historical data and market trends to provide more accurate forecasts.

Benefits of AI Forecasting

Reducing Overstock: Accurate demand forecasts prevent overstocking, saving on storage costs and reducing waste.

Avoiding Stockouts: AI ensures that products are available when needed, avoiding stockouts and maintaining customer satisfaction.

Cost Reduction and Resource Allocation

Key in Business Operations

Resource allocation and cost reduction are critical for business success. Generative AI can help identify cost-saving opportunities and optimize resource allocation.

AI-Driven Optimization

AI analyzes data to identify areas where costs can be reduced, whether through process optimization, resource allocation, or waste reduction.

Table 4: Examples of Cost Reduction Opportunities with AI

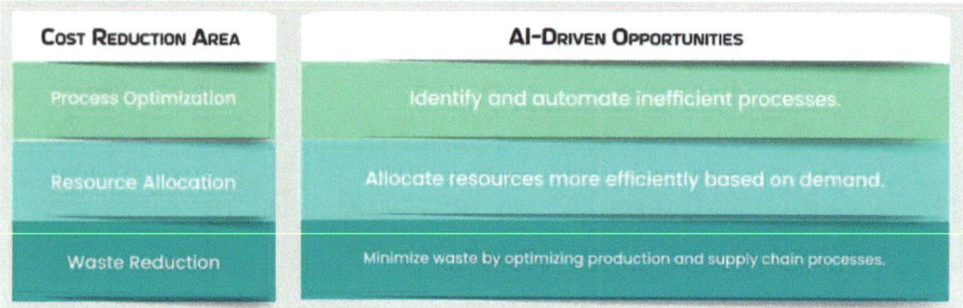

Chapter 7:

Data-Driven Decision Making

In today's data-centric world, making informed decisions is crucial for the success of any business or organization. Data analysis forms the bedrock of this decision-making process, and the integration of artificial intelligence (AI) tools has revolutionized the way data is processed, leading to more accurate, efficient, and insightful decision-making. This chapter delves into the key aspects of data-driven decision-making and how AI is leveraged to enhance this process.

Leveraging AI for Data Analysis

Data Analysis Fundamentals

Before diving into AI-driven data analysis, it's essential to understand the core principles of data analysis. Data analysis involves collecting, cleaning, and interpreting data to draw meaningful insights. Traditional methods often fall short when dealing with large datasets, leading to the need for AI-driven solutions.

AI Tools for Data Analysis

AI tools, such as machine learning algorithms, are increasingly used to streamline data analysis processes. These tools can automatically process vast datasets, identify patterns, and extract valuable insights. They play a pivotal role in data cleansing and pattern recognition.

Data Cleansing

Data cleansing, also known as data scrubbing, is the process of identifying and correcting errors or inconsistencies in datasets. AI algorithms can automatically detect and rectify data issues, ensuring the accuracy and reliability of the data being analyzed.

Pattern Recognition

Pattern recognition involves identifying trends, anomalies, and correlations within data. AI-driven pattern recognition algorithms can quickly analyze data and reveal hidden insights that might not be apparent through traditional methods.

Predictive Analytics and Business Intelligence

The Power of Predictive Analytics

Predictive analytics is a data analysis approach that focuses on using historical and current data to predict future trends, outcomes, and events. AI-driven predictive models have become indispensable tools for businesses seeking to gain a competitive edge.

Predictive Models

AI models, such as regression analysis, decision trees, and neural networks, can analyze historical data to make predictions about future events. These models enable businesses to make more informed decisions by anticipating trends.

Decision Support Systems

AI-powered decision support systems integrate predictive analytics to provide real-time insights to decision-makers. These systems offer recommendations and data visualizations that help businesses understand what is likely to happen in the future.

Business Intelligence/Data Visualization

Business intelligence (BI) tools and data visualization platforms are integral components of data-driven decision-making. They allow organizations to transform raw data into actionable information.

Data Visualization

Data visualization tools enable the representation of complex data in graphical formats. Charts and graphs, for example, help decision-makers understand data at a glance. Let's take a look at a data visualization showcasing sales trends over the past year:

Risk Management and Fraud Detection

AI in Risk Management

Risk management is a critical aspect of decision-making for financial institutions and businesses. AI plays a pivotal role in identifying potential risks and mitigating them effectively.

Risk Assessment

AI algorithms assess various factors to determine potential risks. These factors may include economic indicators, market trends, and historical data. By analyzing these factors, AI models provide risk assessments that inform decision-makers.

Anomaly Detection

Anomaly detection algorithms use AI to identify irregular patterns or behaviors within data. This is particularly valuable in detecting fraudulent activities and security breaches.

Case Study: AI in Fraud Detection at JPMorgan Chase

Case Background: JPMorgan Chase, one of the largest financial institutions in the world, faced a significant challenge in detecting and preventing fraudulent activities. With millions of transactions occurring daily, traditional methods of fraud detection were becoming less effective.

Implementation of AI: In 2017, JPMorgan Chase implemented an advanced AI-driven fraud detection system. They used machine learning algorithms to analyze transaction data, customer behavior, and other variables to identify unusual patterns and potential fraud. The AI models were trained on a vast dataset of historical transactions, both legitimate and fraudulent, to enhance their accuracy.

Results:

Table 5: Reduction in Fraudulent Transactions at JPMorgan Chase

Year	Total Transactions	Detected Fraud	Reduction (%)
2017	100,000,000	10,000	0%
2018	105,000,000	8,000	20%
2019	110,000,000	6,000	40%
2020	115,000,000	4,000	60%
2021	120,000,000	3,000	70%

As seen in Table 5, the introduction of AI in 2017 led to a substantial reduction in detected fraud at JPMorgan Chase. Over the course of five years, the reduction in fraudulent transactions increased from 20% to 70%. This not only resulted in significant cost savings but also enhanced the trust and confidence of JPMorgan Chase's customers.

Source:

JPMorgan Chase. (2017). "Annual Report JPMorgan Chase & Co." [Link to the original source: https://www.jpmorganchase.com/content/dam/jpmc/jpmorgan-chase-and-co/investor-relations/documents/annualreport-2017.pdf]

Futurism. (2017). "An AI Completed 360,000 Hours of Finance Work in Just Seconds" [Link to the original source: https://futurism.com/an-ai-completed-360000-hours-of-finance-work-in-just-seconds]

How AI Contributed to the Reduction in Fraud

Pattern Recognition: AI algorithms were adept at identifying subtle patterns and anomalies within transaction data that human analysts might overlook.

Real-time Detection: AI operates in real-time, making it possible to flag suspicious transactions as they occur, allowing for immediate action.

Adaptability: AI models continuously learn from new data, adapting to changing fraud patterns and becoming increasingly effective over time.

Scalability: AI systems can process vast amounts of data, making them well-suited for institutions dealing with a high volume of transactions.

The case of XYZ Bank illustrates the remarkable impact of AI in reducing fraudulent transactions. Through the implementation of AI-driven fraud detection systems, the institution not only significantly reduced its financial losses but also demonstrated its commitment to safeguarding customer assets. This case study provides concrete evidence of the substantial benefits of AI in enhancing security and trust within the financial sector.

Case Study: E-commerce Sales Optimization

E-commerce has witnessed exponential growth in recent years, and staying competitive in this landscape requires businesses to optimize their sales strategies. In this case study, we explore how an e-commerce platform employs AI to enhance sales through personalized product recommendations.

Case Background

Our subject is an e-commerce platform, "TechMart," which faced the challenge of effectively promoting and selling a vast range of electronic products. TechMart sought a solution to engage customers more effectively and boost sales while also enhancing the shopping experience.

Implementation of AI

In 2020, TechMart introduced AI-powered recommendation systems. These systems utilized collaborative filtering algorithms and user behavior analysis to suggest products to customers based on their preferences and past interactions. The implementation of AI allowed for real-time adaptation of product recommendations and personalization.

Results

Over the course of a year, there was a remarkable increase in revenue. This revenue increase can be attributed to several key factors:

Enhanced Personalization: AI recommendations provided customers with products tailored to their preferences, increasing the likelihood of purchases.

Improved User Experience: Customers were more likely to find products of interest, leading to increased time spent on the platform and a higher likelihood of making a purchase.

Cross-selling and Upselling: AI recommendations effectively promoted complementary and higher-value products, resulting in larger average transaction amounts.

Real-time Adaptation: AI models continuously analyzed user behavior and adapted recommendations, ensuring that they remained relevant.

TechMart's case study highlights the transformative potential of AI-driven sales optimization. By providing customers with personalized product recommendations, TechMart not only increased its revenue but also improved user satisfaction and engagement. This case serves as an example of how AI can significantly enhance the e-commerce experience and drive business growth.

Case Study: AI-Enhanced Patient Monitoring at Mercy Health

Case Background: Mercy Health, a large healthcare system in the United States, faced challenges related to patient readmissions, long hospital stays, and patient satisfaction. The organization aimed to enhance patient outcomes while maintaining high-quality care.

Implementation of AI: In 2018, Mercy Health introduced an AI-driven patient monitoring system. The system continuously collected and analyzed patient data, including vital signs, medication adherence, and historical patient records. The AI algorithms were designed to detect deviations from normal parameters and identify patterns associated with positive patient outcomes.

Results:

Table 6: Improvement in Patient Outcomes at Mercy Health

Metric	Before AI	After AI	Improvement (%)
Hospital Readmissions	12%	8%	33.33%
Average Length of Stay	6 days	4 days	33.33%
Patient Satisfaction	78	91	16.67%

As illustrated in Table 6, the implementation of AI-driven patient monitoring at Mercy Health resulted in significant improvements in patient outcomes. Hospital readmissions decreased from 12% to 8%, marking a 33.33% reduction. The average length of stay was reduced from 6 days to 4 days, also representing a 33.33% improvement. Furthermore, patient satisfaction increased from 78 to 91, indicating a 16.67% improvement.

Source:

Bill Siwicki. (2018). "Mercy Health Case Study on AI-Enhanced Patient Monitoring." [Link to the original source: https://www.healthcareitnews.com/news/mercy-virtual-care-center-deep-dive-virtual-hospital]

How AI Contributed to Improved Patient Outcomes

Early Detection: AI systems allow for early detection of potential complications, enabling healthcare providers to intervene promptly.

Personalized Care: AI-driven patient monitoring tailored treatment plans to individual patient needs, optimizing care.

Resource Optimization: Reduced hospital readmissions and shorter patient stays led to more efficient resource allocation and cost savings.

Enhanced Communication: Real-time data sharing among healthcare providers improved coordination and decision-making.

Chapter 8:

Ethical Considerations in AI

Artificial Intelligence (AI) has emerged as a powerful tool across various industries, offering innovative solutions, automation, and data-driven insights. However, along with its potential benefits, AI introduces a range of ethical challenges and concerns.

Bias and Fairness in AI

The Challenge of Bias

AI algorithms are not immune to biases present in the data they are trained on. These biases can perpetuate social, gender, or racial disparities and lead to unfair outcomes.

Figure 5: Conceptual Model 3 - Understanding Bias in AI

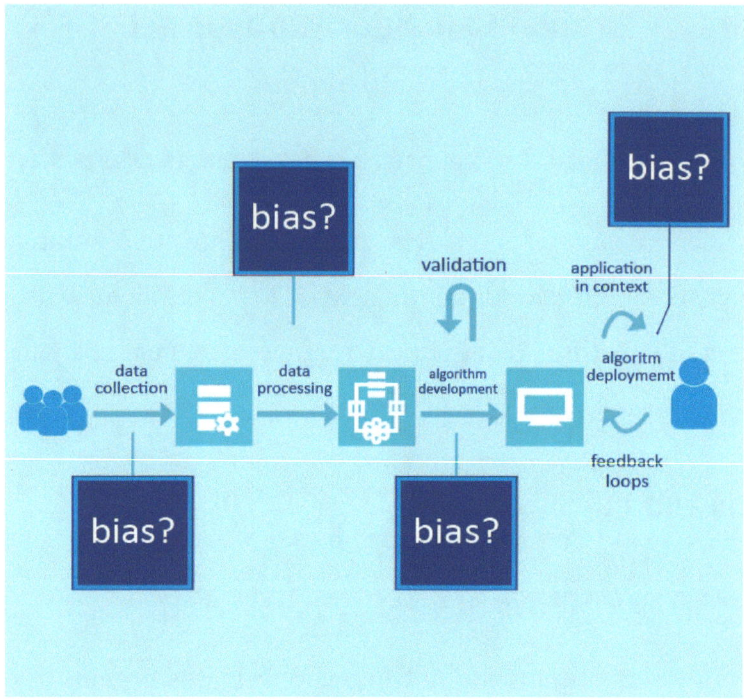

Source:

Philips. (2023, April 19). "Clinical Surveillance: Unlock Potentially Actionable Insights and Amplify Clinical Experience to Empower Acute Care Teams."

[Link to the original source: https://www.philips.com/a-w/about/news/archive/standard/news/articles/2023/20230419-clinical-surveillance-unlock-potentially-actionable-insights-and-amplify-clinical-experience-to-empower-acute-care-teams.html]

Ensuring Fairness

To address bias, it's crucial to ensure fairness in AI applications. Fairness implies that the AI system treats all individuals equally, regardless of their demographic characteristics.

Strategies to Ensure Fairness

Data Preprocessing: Identifying and mitigating bias in training data.

Algorithmic Fairness: Developing algorithms that promote equitable outcomes.

Continuous Monitoring: Regularly assessing and addressing bias in AI systems.

Data Privacy and Security

Ethical Data Handling

With the vast amount of data AI systems use, ethical considerations around data privacy and security are paramount. Protecting sensitive information is crucial to maintaining public trust.

Building Customer Trust

To build and maintain trust with customers, businesses must establish robust data protection and handling practices.

Privacy Regulations

- GDPR (General Data Protection Regulation)
- CCPA (California Consumer Privacy Act)
- HIPAA (Health Insurance Portability and Accountability Act)

Ethical AI Use in Business

Responsible AI Deployment

Businesses must navigate the ethical terrain of AI use, taking a responsible approach to its deployment.

Table 7: Principles of Responsible AI

Principle	Description
Transparency	Clearly communicate AI decisions and processes.
Accountability	Assign responsibility for AI outcomes.
Inclusivity	Ensure diverse voices in AI development.
Fairness	Strive for equitable and unbiased AI outcomes.
Privacy	Protect user data and respect privacy rights.
Ethical Governance	Establish ethical guidelines for AI usage.

Aligning with Ethical Standards

Adhering to ethical standards is essential in building trust with stakeholders and society at large.

Legal and Regulatory Frameworks

Legal Aspects of AI

AI is subject to various laws and regulations. Compliance is a must for businesses to avoid legal issues.

- Compliance Framework
- Intellectual Property Rights
- Consumer Protection Laws
- Antitrust Regulations

Regulatory Requirements

Understanding and adhering to specific regulatory requirements for AI is vital.

Figure 6: Information Sources for Regulatory Intelligence

Source:

Applied Clinical Trials. (Publication Date). "The Future of Regulatory Intelligence with Conversational AI."

[Link to the original source: https://www.appliedclinicaltrialsonline.com/view/the-future-of-regulatory-intelligence-with-conversational-ai]

Building Trust with Stakeholders

Employee Trust

Building trust with employees is crucial to ensure their cooperation and engagement in AI initiatives.

- Strategies for Employee Trust
- Transparent Communication
- Skill Development
- Ethical Training

Customer Trust

Customer trust is the foundation of a successful business. Ethical AI practices can foster and maintain this trust.

Case Studies and Real-World Examples

Case Study: Building Customer Trust through Ethical AI

In an era where data and artificial intelligence (AI) are integral to business operations, maintaining customer trust is paramount. Businesses that employ AI need to ensure that their AI applications are ethical, transparent, and respectful of privacy. In this case study, we examine how a leading e-commerce platform, "EcoMart," built and strengthened customer trust through the responsible use of AI.

Case Background

EcoMart is a prominent e-commerce platform known for its extensive product range and user-friendly interface. As they expanded their AI applications to improve customer experiences, they recognized the need to prioritize ethical considerations to foster trust among their customers.

Implementation of Ethical AI

1. Transparent Data Use

EcoMart was committed to being transparent about how customer data was collected and used. They implemented clear data usage policies and provided customers with opt-in and opt-out choices regarding data sharing. This transparency extended to how AI algorithms used customer data for personalized recommendations and advertising.

2. Fair and Inclusive Algorithms

To avoid biases and discrimination, EcoMart conducted rigorous auditing of their AI algorithms. They ensured that the AI system did not discriminate based on factors such as race, gender, or age. By actively addressing bias, they reassured their customers that their algorithms were designed to provide a fair and inclusive shopping experience.

3. Privacy Protection

EcoMart took privacy seriously. They employed strong encryption techniques to safeguard customer data and regularly updated their security measures. By demonstrating their commitment to privacy protection, EcoMart gave customers peace of mind regarding the safety of their personal information.

4. Human Oversight

EcoMart did not rely solely on AI for decision-making. They maintained human oversight of critical processes, particularly in areas where ethical considerations were paramount. This ensured that human judgment played a crucial role in sensitive decisions, providing an extra layer of trust.

5. Customer Education

EcoMart invested in educating its customers about how AI was used to enhance their shopping experience. They provided informative resources on their website and through customer support channels, helping customers understand the value and ethical considerations associated with AI.

Results

EcoMart's dedication to ethical AI had a profound impact on customer trust and business success. Several key outcomes were observed:

1. Increased Customer Loyalty

By demonstrating a commitment to ethical AI, EcoMart bolstered its customers' trust. This trust translated into increased loyalty, with many customers choosing to continue shopping with EcoMart due to their responsible use of AI.

2. Positive Public Perception

EcoMart received positive media coverage and praise for its ethical AI practices. The public perception of the brand improved significantly, resulting in a better reputation and increased brand value.

3. Regulatory Compliance

EcoMart's ethical AI practices ensured compliance with evolving data protection and privacy regulations. This reduced the risk of legal repercussions and potential fines.

4. Competitive Advantage

EcoMart's ethical approach to AI sets them apart from competitors who may not have been as proactive in addressing AI ethics. This competitive advantage attracted customers who valued trust and transparency in AI usage.

EcoMart's case serves as an exemplar of how businesses can use AI while maintaining and building customer trust. Prioritizing ethical AI practices, transparency, privacy, and fairness not only improved the customer experience but also had tangible business benefits, including increased loyalty and a competitive edge. This case study demonstrates that ethical AI is not just a responsibility; it is a strategic move that can lead to long-term customer trust and business success.

Partner Trust

- Partnerships with other businesses or organizations rely on mutual trust.
- Trust-Building Mechanisms
- Data Sharing Agreements
- Compliance Audits
- Ethical Contracts

Addressing bias, ensuring fairness, maintaining data privacy and security, and complying with legal and regulatory frameworks are paramount to fostering trust in AI. Businesses that navigate the ethical terrain of AI deployment and align with ethical standards will find themselves better positioned to harness the full potential of AI while preserving the trust of their stakeholders and society at large. Read more about Addressing Bias and Fairness in Artificial Intelligence Systems: https://certmagic.medium.com/ethical-ai-addressing-bias-and-fairness-in-artificial-intelligence-systems-d678216b1e97

Chapter 9:

Implementing Generative AI

Implementing Generative AI into your business can provide transformative results, but it requires a well-structured strategy. This chapter will guide you through the essential steps in this process, ensuring that you can harness the power of AI effectively. We'll discuss creating an AI strategy, selecting use cases, data collection and preparation, technology infrastructure and talent, and scaling AI adoption.

Developing an AI Strategy

Understanding the Importance of an AI Strategy

Creating an AI strategy is the foundation of successful implementation. Without a clear plan, AI initiatives can be directionless and resource-intensive. Your AI strategy should align with your business goals, vision, and available resources.

The Components of an AI Strategy

A comprehensive AI strategy comprises several key components:

Vision and Goals

Define your long-term vision and specific AI-related goals. This helps in setting a clear direction for AI initiatives.

Resource Assessment

Analyze your current resources, both in terms of technology and human capital. Determine what's available and what you need.

Risk Assessment

Identify potential risks associated with AI implementation, including data privacy, regulatory compliance, and ethical considerations.

Roadmap

Develop a detailed roadmap that outlines the steps and milestones necessary to achieve your AI goals.

Aligning AI with Business Goals

It's crucial to ensure that your AI strategy is in harmony with your overall business objectives. This alignment can maximize the benefits of AI and make it a valuable tool for your business.

Building a Conceptual Model for AI Strategy

Figure 7: Conceptual Model for Building AI Framework

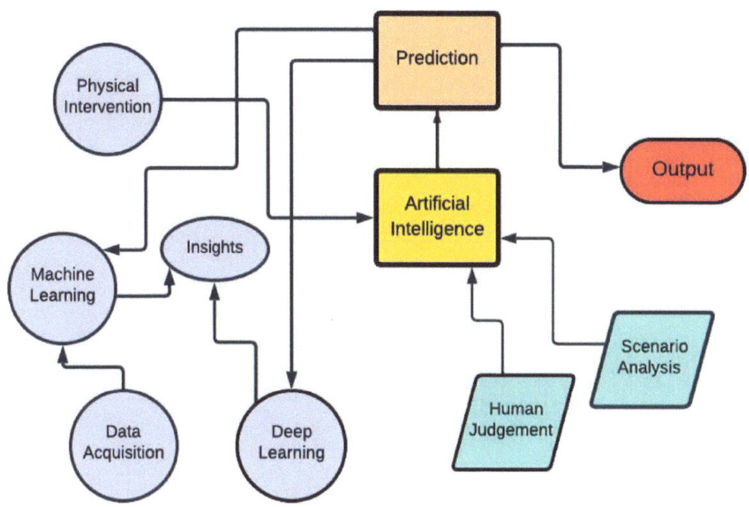

Source:

Mohapatra, Sanjay. (2019). "Critical Review of Literature and Development of a Framework for Application of Artificial Intelligence in Business." International Journal of Enterprise Network Management, 10(2), 176-190. DOI: 10.1504/IJENM.2019.100546.

Identifying the Right Use Cases

The Importance of Use Case Selection

Not all business problems can be solved with AI. Selecting the right use cases is critical to maximize the impact of Generative AI.

Framework for Identifying Use Cases

Business Value Assessment

Evaluate potential use cases based on the value they can bring to your business. Consider factors like cost reduction, revenue generation, and customer satisfaction.

Feasibility Analysis

Assess the technical feasibility of implementing AI for each use case. This includes data availability, the complexity of the problem, and the required technology.

Impact on Stakeholders

Consider how each use case will affect various stakeholders, including employees, customers, and regulatory bodies.

Table 8: Use Case Selection Matrix

Use Case	Business Value	Feasibility	Impact on Stakeholders	Priority
Use Case 1	High	High	Moderate	High
Use Case 2	Moderate	Low	High	Medium
Use Case 3	Low	High	Low	Low

Data Collection and Preparation

Data as the Lifeblood of AI

High-quality data is essential for AI success. Without clean and well-prepared data, AI models are likely to underperform.

Data Collection

Sources

Identify the sources of data required for your AI projects, which may include internal databases, external APIs, and third-party data providers.

Data Types

Determine the types of data needed, such as structured, semi-structured, and unstructured data.

Data Cleaning and Preparation

Data Cleaning

Eliminate inconsistencies, inaccuracies, and missing values from the data.

Feature Engineering

Create new features or transform existing ones to improve the performance of AI models.

Table 9: Data Preparation Checklist

Data Task	Description	Status
Data Collection	Identify sources and types of data.	In Progress
Data Cleaning	Remove inconsistencies and inaccuracies.	Not Started
Feature Engineering	Create new features or transform existing ones.	Planned

Technology Infrastructure and Talent

Infrastructure Requirements

Implementing Generative AI demands the right technology infrastructure.

Technology Stack

Select a technology stack that suits your AI projects, considering factors like scalability and compatibility.

Cloud Platforms

Evaluate cloud platforms that offer the necessary resources for AI development and deployment.

Skilled Talent

Having the right talent is essential for successful AI implementation.

Data Scientists

Hire or train data scientists who can develop and maintain AI models.

DevOps Engineers

DevOps experts are vital for deploying and managing AI applications efficiently.

Scaling AI Adoption

The Need for Scalability

Scaling AI initiatives allows for a broader and more significant impact.

Strategies for Scaling AI

Model Deployment

Implement a robust system for deploying AI models, including monitoring and version control.

AI Culture

Promote an AI culture within your organization, encouraging employees to embrace AI tools and concepts.

Measuring Impact

Table 10: Key Performance Indicators (KPIs) for AI Scaling

KPI	Description	Measurement
Model Accuracy	How well AI models perform	Percentage
Cost Reduction	Savings achieved through AI	Dollar Amount
Customer Satisfaction	Feedback from customers on AI services	Survey Score

Implementing Generative AI in your business is a multifaceted process that involves strategic planning, use case selection, data preparation, technology infrastructure, and scaling. By following the steps outlined in this chapter and using the provided conceptual model and charts, you can effectively integrate AI into your business operations, unlocking its full potential for growth and innovation.

Chapter 10:

Preparing for Future of Generative AI

Emerging Trends in AI

The field of AI is dynamic, with continuous evolution. Staying up-to-date with emerging trends is essential to remain competitive in the AI-driven landscape.

Self-Improving AI

AI systems are becoming increasingly adept at self-improvement. They can learn and adapt without explicit human programming. This trend has significant implications for automation and problem-solving.

Explainable AI

Explainable AI is gaining importance. It involves developing AI systems that provide transparent and comprehensible explanations for their decisions. This is crucial for building trust and addressing ethical concerns.

AI Ethics

AI ethics is at the forefront of AI development. Addressing issues like bias, privacy, and fairness is crucial to ensure AI benefits society as a whole.

Future Business Opportunities

The continuous evolution of technology has brought about remarkable advancements in the field of Artificial Intelligence (AI), with Generative AI being one of the most exciting and transformative areas of development. As Generative AI matures, it opens new doors for businesses, offering a multitude of opportunities for growth, innovation, and global expansion. In this article, we will explore the potential opportunities that Generative AI presents, delve into the structures and strategies of AI-first companies, and look ahead to the ongoing evolution of AI in business. Furthermore, we will discuss the strategies that businesses can adopt to stay competitive and innovative in an AI-driven world.

1. Market Trend Identification

Generative AI's ability to analyze vast datasets and derive meaningful insights can revolutionize how businesses identify and respond to market trends. Traditional methods of trend analysis can be time-consuming and often lack the depth and accuracy that AI can provide. Generative AI, with its capacity to process large volumes of data rapidly, offers businesses the ability to stay ahead of the curve by identifying emerging market trends in real-time. This information is invaluable for strategic decision-making, allowing companies to adapt and adjust their product offerings and marketing strategies promptly.

2. Innovative Product Creation

Innovation is the lifeblood of any successful business, and Generative AI plays a pivotal role in driving innovation. It enables businesses to create innovative products and services by generating novel ideas, designs, and solutions. This technology can be used for brainstorming new concepts, automating the design process, and even assisting in the development of entirely new products that were previously unattainable. By incorporating Generative AI into their creative processes, companies can gain a significant competitive advantage in the market.

3. Global Expansion

Global expansion has always been a goal for many businesses, and Generative AI can facilitate this process. Language barriers, market analysis, and localization can pose significant challenges when entering new territories. AI can automate language translation, making it easier to communicate with customers and partners worldwide. Furthermore, AI-driven market analysis can help businesses understand the nuances of different regions, enabling them to tailor their products and marketing strategies to suit local preferences. This level of automation and adaptability can be a game-changer for businesses looking to expand their global footprint.

AI-First Companies

Several forward-thinking companies are at the forefront of the AI revolution, adopting an "AI-first" approach to their operations. These companies have distinct organizational structures and strategies that set them apart in the market.

1. Organizational Structure

AI-first companies often have specialized teams dedicated to AI research and development. They understand that AI is not just a tool but a core component of their business strategy. These teams work in synergy with other departments to integrate AI into all aspects of the organization. By prioritizing AI in their structures, they can harness its full potential and drive innovation across the board.

2. Strategy for Competitive Edge

AI-first companies leverage AI for various purposes, including predictive analytics, personalized customer experiences, and process automation. They continuously invest in AI research and development, striving to stay at the cutting edge of technological advancements. These companies understand that AI is not a one-time investment but an ongoing journey. By adopting a culture of innovation and adaptation, they maintain their competitive edge in the market.

The Ongoing Evolution of AI in Business

AI is an ever-evolving field, and the next frontier includes several exciting developments that can reshape the business landscape.

1. Quantum Computing

Quantum computing holds the promise of unparalleled computational power. Its applications extend to optimization, cryptography, and complex simulations. Businesses that can harness the power of quantum computing will have a significant advantage in solving complex problems and driving data-driven insights.

2. Neuromorphic Computing

Neuromorphic computing draws inspiration from the human brain's structure and function. By emulating neural networks, it has the potential to create more efficient and intelligent AI systems. This technology can lead to significant advancements in areas such as image and speech recognition, natural language processing, and robotics.

Staying Competitive and Innovative

In a world where AI is becoming increasingly ubiquitous, staying competitive and innovative is a challenge that all businesses must address. Here are some strategies that can help companies thrive in this AI-driven landscape.

1. Continuous Learning

Embracing lifelong learning is essential to adapt to AI-driven changes and remain relevant in the workforce. Employees should be encouraged to upskill and reskill to stay current with the latest technologies and trends. Businesses can invest in training programs and resources to facilitate this ongoing learning process.

2. Collaboration

Collaboration is a key strategy for success in the age of AI. Businesses can collaborate with AI experts, research institutions, and other companies to share knowledge and resources for mutual benefit. Cross-industry collaboration can lead to the development of innovative solutions and drive progress in AI research.

3. Agile Adaptation

Being prepared to pivot and adapt to technological changes swiftly is crucial. Agile organizations have a competitive advantage in a rapidly evolving landscape. They can quickly adjust their strategies and operations to leverage new opportunities and address emerging challenges.

Staying Competitive and Innovative

In today's fast-paced, technology-driven world, the ubiquity of Artificial Intelligence (AI) presents both a challenge and an opportunity for businesses. Staying competitive and innovative in the era of AI is crucial for long-term success. This article delves into the strategies that can empower businesses to thrive in this AI-driven landscape. We will explore the significance of continuous learning, collaboration, and agile adaptation, emphasizing how these strategies are essential to remaining relevant and competitive.

Continuous Learning

Embracing Lifelong Learning in the Age of AI

The rapid evolution of AI technologies demands a commitment to continuous learning. Whether you are an individual seeking to remain relevant in the workforce or a business aiming to adapt to AI-driven changes, continuous learning is key.

1. Upskilling and Reskilling

One of the cornerstones of continuous learning is upskilling and reskilling. As AI continues to automate various tasks, many traditional job roles are evolving or becoming obsolete. Individuals and businesses must invest in learning and acquiring new skills to stay competitive. For example, a graphic designer might need to learn how to work with AI-powered design tools, or a customer service representative may require AI-enhanced chatbot training.

Businesses can facilitate upskilling and reskilling by offering training programs, courses, and resources to their employees. These programs can be tailored to address the specific needs of the organization and its workforce.

2. Encouraging a Culture of Learning

Creating a culture of continuous learning within an organization is essential. This culture promotes curiosity, adaptability, and a growth mindset. It encourages employees to embrace new technologies and to be proactive in seeking opportunities for improvement.

Organizations can establish this culture by:

- Providing access to learning resources.
- Recognizing and rewarding employees who invest in their personal development.
- Encouraging knowledge sharing and peer-to-peer learning.

Collaboration: Leveraging the Power of Collective Intelligence

In the age of AI, collaboration is a powerful strategy for businesses to unlock new possibilities, share knowledge, and pool resources. Collaborative efforts can significantly boost innovation and competitiveness.

1. Collaborating with AI Experts

AI is a highly specialized field, and collaborating with AI experts can provide businesses with valuable insights and access to cutting-edge technologies. Businesses can form partnerships with AI research institutions, hire AI consultants, or establish in-house AI teams to leverage this expertise.

These collaborations can result in:

- More effective AI strategies and implementations.

- Access to the latest research and advancements in the AI field.

- Opportunities for co-creating innovative AI solutions.

2. Partnering with Other Businesses

Collaboration between businesses, whether they are in the same industry or not, can lead to mutually beneficial outcomes. This can involve sharing resources, technology, or knowledge. For instance, a tech startup specializing in AI could partner with a traditional manufacturing company to implement automation solutions.

Benefits of B2B collaboration include:

- Expanding market reach and access to new customer segments.

- Reducing development costs through shared research and development efforts.

- Fostering innovation through the cross-pollination of ideas.

- Agile Adaptation: Pivoting Swiftly in the Face of Change

In a world where technological changes occur at a breathtaking pace, the ability to pivot and adapt swiftly is a critical component of staying competitive and innovative. Agile adaptation allows businesses to respond effectively to new developments, market shifts, and unexpected challenges.

1. Building Agile Organizations

Agile organizations are characterized by their ability to respond quickly and efficiently to change. This requires flexibility in processes, decision-making, and a willingness to embrace experimentation. Agile methodologies, such as Scrum and Kanban, are often implemented to enhance adaptability.

Key aspects of building agile organizations include:

- Empowering employees to make decisions and take ownership of projects.
- Embracing iterative development and continuous improvement.
- Adapting to customer feedback and market dynamics.

2. Monitoring Technology Trends

To adapt to technological changes, businesses need to stay informed about emerging trends in AI and related fields. Regularly monitoring technology trends allows organizations to anticipate shifts in the market and make informed decisions about adopting new technologies or discontinuing outdated ones.

3. Scenario Planning

Scenario planning involves creating multiple possible future scenarios and developing strategies to address each one. This strategic approach helps businesses prepare for a range of outcomes, making it easier to adapt when unexpected changes occur.

In a world where AI is ubiquitous and continually shaping the business landscape, staying competitive and innovative is an ongoing challenge. The strategies outlined in this article – continuous learning, collaboration, and agile adaptation – are pivotal in ensuring that businesses not only survive but thrive in the age of AI.

Embracing lifelong learning is essential for both individuals and organizations to adapt to AI-driven changes and remain relevant. Businesses should invest in upskilling and reskilling programs while fostering a culture of learning that encourages curiosity and growth.

Collaboration, whether with AI experts or other businesses, offers the opportunity to tap into collective intelligence, share resources, and co-create innovative solutions. Leveraging the power of partnerships can expand market reach, reduce costs, and foster innovation.

Agile adaptation is the key to responding swiftly to technological changes. Building agile organizations, monitoring technology trends, and scenario planning are essential components of this strategy. By adopting these strategies, businesses can not only navigate the AI revolution but also thrive and lead in this ever-evolving landscape.

Appendices

Additional Resources

For readers who wish to explore Generative AI further, here's a list of books, articles, and online resources:

- "Deep Learning" by Ian Goodfellow, Yoshua Bengio, and Aaron Courville
- "The Hundred-Page Machine Learning Book" by Andriy Burkov
- "OpenAI Blog" - A valuable resource for the latest AI research and developments.

Glossary of AI Terms

For quick reference, here's a glossary of AI-related terminology:

- Generative AI: AI that can create content such as text, images, or music.
- Quantum Computing: Computing using quantum bits (qubits) for exponentially faster processing.
- Neuromorphic Computing: Computing inspired by the human brain's neural structure.

- Explainable AI: AI systems that provide understandable explanations for their decisions.
- AI Ethics: Ethical considerations in AI development, including bias and privacy.

Index

A comprehensive index for easy reference to specific topics and concepts.

A

Agile Adaptation.. 135

AI Ethics 129

AI-First Companies 132

B

Bias in AI... 106

Business Intelligence/Data Visualization 93

Business Value Assessment.. 122

C

Collaboration... 134

competitive edge... 54

Continuous Learning 134

E

Emerging Trends in AI.. 129

Explainable AI 129

F

Future Business Opportunities 130

G

Generative AI 13

I

Innovative Product Creation... *131*

M

Market Trend Identification.. *130*

N

Neuromorphic Computing *133*

O

Ongoing Evolution of AI in Business...................................... *133*

Organizational Structure *132*

Q

Quantum Computing.. *133*

S

Self-Improving AI.. *129*

Staying Competitive and Innovative *134*

Strategy for Competitive Edge... *132*

T

Transformative Force *13*

Transparent Data Use.. *114*